A Garden Gallery

ONE CANNOT CREATE BEAUTY; ONE CAN ONLY CREATE CIRCUMSTANCES FAVORABLE TO IT.

—Rainer Maria Rilke

A
Garden Gallery

*The Plants,
Art, and Hardscape of
Little and Lewis*

George Little and David Lewis

PHOTOGRAPHY BY **Barbara Denk** | FOREWORD BY **Ketzel Levine**

TIMBER PRESS
Portland · Cambridge

For Joanne and Robert Lewis:
She, whose soaring spirit became a world-conscience; and he, upright man who,
even now in my sixties, became the Good Father.

And for David who encouraged my heart once more to be joyful.

—G.L.

To my father and mother who taught me to see beauty,
and to George who helped me to embrace it.

—D.L.

contents

FOREWORD

I'VE RACKED MY BRAIN TRYING TO FIND some elegant way to say this—to use a language suffused with the wonder, magic, and sense of mystery that lie at the heart of this book—but it seems I am of blunter stuff, so I'll give it to you straight:

The hell with my own innate creativity. If I had the cash, I'd just put down the shovel and buy a Little and Lewis garden. I'd say, Guys, it's yours. Make me a world. Wake me when the dream begins.

I realize this is a hideous thing to say. As gardeners, we are exhorted endlessly to express ourselves in the garden. And believe me, I have tried, with some degree of success. I've discovered what plants delight me, I've introduced levity through garden art, and I've embraced orange, chartreuse, and bizarre brown leaves in an effort to speak my mind. I even have bubbling water, a dramatically painted wall, and a concrete urn stuffed with otherworldly, fleshy succulents. In other words, I have all the fundamental elements of a Little and Lewis garden. But I don't have the touch.

Something divine happens to me when I visit George Little and David Lewis's garden on Bainbridge Island, in the middle of

Washington State's Puget Sound. I have this sense that I am exactly where I am meant to be. Seduced by the sound of dripping, trickling, rushing water, I suspend all chatter in my head and submit to impossibilities.

Consider this scene: A huge, indigo-blue basin is filled with water. Its surface is constantly moving in perfect concentric circles, stirred by slow drops of rain that fall from the sky. Just one problem: It's not raining! The weather's gorgeous! In fact, the drops are falling from an overhanging tree limb, fitted with a length of well-camouflaged hose.

Clever, sure. But the effect is inspired. Rather than feeling tricked, one feels cajoled, included, and invited to play.

And here is the playground: emerald banana leaves emerging from turquoise-washed ruins; a baby-teared tree that weeps; cracked dinosaur eggs that bubble with water; leaves the colors of sunrise. A Little and Lewis garden is a giddy, sacred place where everything can happen, where life is blessed and sweet. Where time stands still and the senses are allowed to wander.

I hate them. It's not fair.

My question, to both David and George, is this: Who told you anything was possible? Who said you could have so much fun? And why is it that some of us just grow plants, while you create entire worlds with leaves?

My imagined answer from them is this: We crave beauty. (I imagine this answer fully aware of David's penchant for bad TV.) Craving beauty would explain a lot about the look and feel of their garden, because it aims so much higher than being pretty. The Little and Lewis garden wants to create an atmosphere in which acts of faith are possible, where you can turn a corner and discover your own sense of wonder—as well as sadness, and longing, and loss.

I feel all these things in their garden—would that I felt only the blessed and sweet!—yet I have never felt manipulated by the crafty hands of the gardeners. I experience the illusion that the discoveries I make there are all my own. I don't know how they do that, keep surprises fresh and hope abundant. I don't know how their placement of plant and pot turns into a sweet feeling, a cherished memory, a desire to find more joy in my life.

I only know that when my muse isn't talking and my garden has nothing to say, I imagine myself in an ancient glade bathed in light, color, and mystery. I conjure up the atmosphere of a Little and Lewis garden, and in their world I find my own permission to dream.

—KETZEL LEVINE

The Spirit in the Woods plaque, inspired by a line from Wordsworth, and *Hedychium* 'Pink V'.

introduction

[D a v i d]

SHORTLY AFTER I MOVED TO THE NORTHWEST in the late 1980s, I purchased a small concrete fountain for my new home from a local sculptor, George Little. I later invited him to my house to see how I had placed his work of art in my front yard. "It's nice," he said, "but that fountain pool is too small. We need to make it bigger!"

The following weekend, George helped me dig out my small 3- by 5-foot pool and expand it to 5 by 12 feet. It became a huge focal point—in fact, the only focal point of my budding garden. We had such a great time working together, we quickly became friends and decided to go into business designing and creating fountains, pools, and ponds. We placed a small advertisement in the local newspaper, and within six months, we both had quit our day jobs and were working full time on our new vocation.

Our entry gate shaded by a dark smoke tree (*Cotinus*); the sphere was made by filling a small beach ball with concrete.

George continued to sculpt and create new works of art while mentoring me in concrete techniques and pool design. With each new pool or artwork installation, our reputation grew, especially for the artwork. After a few short years we realized that digging holes was not our first love, and we decided to put all our energy into sculpting. Today, except for an occasional design consultation, we spend nearly all our time in the sculpting studio and in our own garden.

Over the past thirteen years, George and I have worked closely together, establishing our rhythm and gaining an understanding of each other's personality. We have learned to balance our workloads and responsibilities. We have accepted, or adapted to, each other's foibles and have learned to compromise. For example, when we sat down to write this manuscript we soon realized that we both wanted to be "heard" in our own words, unencumbered by the traditional one-author format. As a result, we have written this book in two voices, and the compromise has produced a truer and more reflective story. It has allowed our individual personalities and styles to weave together the story of our collaboration.

For two artists to work together on nearly everything is rare. We sign both our names to every piece that comes out of our studio, regardless of the amount of time that each of us put into its creation. When we lecture to groups, we do so together, playing off each other's words and ideas to form a fluid presentation. Our styles and interests are different, but the blend of our skills, personalities, and passions creates a single entity: Little and Lewis.

[G e o r g e]

As a very young person—over fifty years ago now—I had an interest in gardening and, in particular, water in the garden. One of my first attempts at water gardening was to dig a five-foot-long trench in the backyard, line it with aluminum foil, and proudly show our new "stream" to my parents. They were very kind. But some of my strongest

Water-loving *Lysimachia punctata* 'Alexander' atop our mossy Egyptian column fountain.

early memories are of planting spring flowers in a rock garden with my parents. The earthy smells and the moist feel of the freshening air of the season became part of why I garden. I was and still am enraptured by the sensuousness of the outdoors, by its vastness, and by the timeless quality of living as part of nature.

At the same time, I developed an early attraction to the mysterious atmosphere that hangs over the ruins of ancient cultures: The remains of Egypt, Greece, and Rome made my hair stand on end. I once saw a photo of ruined-looking Greek or Roman columns in a magazine of my mother's. Their stature, textures, and faded colors fascinated me. The columns had grasses growing from the tops, and I thought: That's for me! I wanted to try to replicate the feeling those columns gave me. It was many years, however, before I was able to bring together these long-held passions for ancient-looking architecture, gardening, and water. By the time David and I met, I had had years of experience in concrete sculpting and watercolor painting. But the old interests had always stayed with me, and one day, while David and I were enlarging the existing small pool in his garden, it was as if those early ideas awoke and it was the time to make them happen.

So we made our first concrete column. It was clunky and square, but we loved it. At a stately eight feet tall, with color washes that looked weather-worn, right away it gave the garden a completely different feel. It was a moment of celebration for us. We knew our direction.

David and I had a great time working together on those first projects. We shared similar enthusiasms: We both had an effusive sense of color; we both had a passion for tropical plants and for ancient-looking architecture; we both loved water. I think we knew then that we had found work we could do for years to come. And that is, indeed, the way

How does the calla (here, *Zantedeschia aethiopica*) manage to be both majestic and playful at once?

it has been. Apart from the rare times when we stubbornly disagree or become temperamental, we work well together. Ideas for techniques, inspirations for sculpture designs, and feelings for color flow back and forth, from one of us to the other, in a fluid way that gives us pleasure and makes us a living. We perceive the whole thing as a blessing, and we are very grateful.

[George and David]

This book is about sharing a very personal gardening style and visual approach. It illustrates years of our collaborative endeavor in transforming a nondescript space of grass into a garden that is visited by people from around the world. But it also represents our effort to inspire, to encourage readers to rely on their own imaginations in much the same way. A true gardener, one who is curious and loves to share ideas, will discreetly peek in over the hedge or fence of a neighbor's garden to see what they are doing, get ideas, and awaken his or her own creativity. This is your invitation to peek over our fence.

Little & Lewis

The central court and pergola with its 8-foot columns; *Canna* 'Tropicana' grows large in planters while leaf sculptures anchor at lower right.

CHAPTER ONE

gardening from within

PARTNERING WITH NATURE
[George]

WHEN I STEP OUT INTO THE GARDEN in the morning, the first thing I usually do is take a deep breath—taste the air. It tells me a lot about what the day is shaping up to be. It gets the garden's weather inside me more deeply. I feel that every garden has its own distinct atmosphere that carries the personality of the garden and its creator. This atmosphere is, of course, in the garden spaces, not in the individual plants and sculpture. So the air around things is just as vital as the things themselves. That thought imbues the idea of space with presence—an energy felt in the air of a good garden that seems as real as the garden itself. It gives voice to the personality of the place. Some day, simply stand in your garden and listen. Or walk among the beds, just to enjoy, but remain attentive. It's always amazing to me what comes: A great many of our ideas for sculpture, fountains, and plantings have come from being open in this way to our garden's spaces. The contemplative frame of mind achieved by being attentive, whether sitting or walking, often

Our front porch features an emerging canna and *Hydrangea* 'Bluebird'; the Fossils plaque hangs on the wall.

gives an inner stillness that helps one to perceive the voice of the garden. It certainly gives rise to a sense of connectedness that is itself
delightful. And so we can actually have a dialog with our garden, working with it to make a oneness discovered like something new, though it
is as old as the stones we uncover when digging. A large part of the
delight found in a good garden is in that quality: feelings both ancient
and new, dark and bright, sensed in the heart and gut—no need to
think them out.

Trust yourself. If you try to make gardening a kind of intellectual
exercise, or are primarily concerned with what someone might think of
your efforts, you may end up forcing your garden's personality. You

Below: A hand-painted, concrete gunnera leaf. **Right**: Two Morning Glory vessels, one with sedum and a blue mirror ball, the other with bright cerise petunia, and *Crocosmia* 'Lucifer' all around.

sharing the garden

One benefit of having a garden is being able to share all your hard work and creative endeavors with your community. Every year we open our garden to select tours for local and national horticulture organizations. Each group sponsors its tour and receives an admission donation from visitors. It's a great fundraiser for the group, and we especially enjoy interacting with visitors who have a common interest and cause. Occasionally, if it's an organization with which we feel strongly affiliated, we offer a more tailored event in our garden, such as a small private dinner or afternoon tea, as a donation for their auction.

But you don't necessarily have to throw open the doors to your private garden retreat! There are other ways to share your garden or give back to your community through your gardening hobby. Donate old garden books to a local library so that others can learn from the wealth of knowledge they provide. Volunteer your time in a neighbor's garden where the owner, perhaps, needs a little bit of help or encouragement. Or volunteer to help with a local public school, or other nonprofit garden. Best of all is sharing any excess plants and flowers. As you thin out your plants, pot some up and give them as gifts or as donations to a local horticulture society's plant sale. And a beautiful bouquet of fresh flowers—although it can be very difficult to cut flowers from your garden—always makes a wonderful personal gift.

Left: *Epiphyllum* 'Deutsche Kaiserin'.
Right: *Solanum quitoense* at center with a little mandarin orange.

can always tell when someone is trying too hard. It just doesn't work. And lot size, sculptures, money—none of these matters much in making a real garden. What matters is the relation of people to their spaces. Does the garden seem a natural extension of the owner? Is there a love of gardening here, a simple joy in the partnering with nature to make something beautiful?

THE ART OF GARDENING TOGETHER
[David]

The relationship between you and your garden is a lot like that between you and another person. To weave common paths, we practice the virtues of understanding, patience, and giving. In return the garden

Left: A potted Bowles Golden Sedge, *Carex elata* 'Aurea', in a long pool which is set with dripping columns. **Right**: We gingerly repot a bad-tempered agave and make new homes for a few of its pups.

rewards us with the gifts of beauty, companionship, and knowledge. But all that can change when you actually share your garden relationship with another person and a potential *ménage à trois* develops.

There is a fine art to gardening with another person. I would like to imagine that it is a beautiful balance of give and take, compromise, and lovingly granting the wishes and vision of that other person. In reality, it is often stubborn reluctance, quiet moping, or raised voices among the plants we love. George and I have been gardening together for many years, and although we have gotten used to each other's style and methods of introducing change, the process still calls up our stubbornness. As a matter of principle I will often reject George's planting suggestions even before he has finished his sentence. He is used to that and knows that eventually I will give in. I know I will too, but I find it important to resist a little to satisfy my need for control. We put up with a lot from each other, but with mutual admiration.

Recently George has resorted to more mischievous and less confrontational ways to make changes in the garden. Some of our biggest disagreements are over the removal of existing plantings. It's nearly impossible for me to pull out or get rid of a plant, regardless of its poor health or inappropriate location. Once, when we disagreed over whether to remove a towering wisteria that was climbing high into a tree and slowly smothering it, he secretly severed it at the base, piled dirt around the cut, and left the plant in place. A month later the wisteria was dead—and I always assumed it was from natural causes. In hindsight, that was a brilliant way to achieve a much-needed sacrifice. Now, when George is determined to remove an offending plant, he skips the tedious, sometimes acrimonious method of trying to convince me, and sends me out on errands instead. While I am gone he

Another gunnera sculpture, cast from a living leaf and washed in lime greens, is perched on our small Tuscan column.

unceremoniously removes the plant and assumes that I won't notice. I do immediately, but I don't comment until several weeks have passed, thus giving him the pleasure of his waywardness. He doesn't know I am onto his new trick. Besides, as hard as it is to admit, his changes and plant cullings always improve the garden.

Gardening with a partner is at the best of times a very natural and gratifying process. We encourage each other to take on the responsibilities of the garden that bring us enjoyment, and we try to keep the work fun. George likes to water, so the chore of watering the garden falls to him. For him, it is a contemplative task, and he often creates ideas for sculpture and studio projects as he slowly moves around with the garden hose trailing behind him. In summer it can sometimes take two hours or more per day to water our garden, as it is all done by hand except for the occasional use of a movable overhead sprinkler. This method of watering, as opposed to an automatic irrigation system, allows one to be more present in the garden as a whole as well as more able to watch and tend plants in need of individual care.

I enjoy weeding, tidying, and staking plants (my constant need to control extends even to nature). I too will use this quiet, methodical time in the garden to dream and plan. The more strenuous projects of planting and moving soil or compost are shared—often with minimal verbal direction, since we have worked side by side for so many years. We each accept the work, grateful for the garden that is created in the process.

The division of responsibilities is even more evident in our studio. George provides the creative fuel. I manage the business. I watch and admire his creative process, as he produces an endless stream of new sculpture designs and ideas, many of which sit unexplored in folders

The Bocca di Veritas Fountain—modeled after Rome's—overhung with *Hydrangea quercifolia* on the left and a white *Filipendula vulgaris* 'Flore Pleno' to the right.

and sketch pads. There is simply not enough time. I've learned that the creative process is fluid and abstract and cannot be controlled. My role is to bring a sense of order and reality to the business, based on numbers and schedules. Although our different styles can conflict, the balance they create gives each of us a knowledge of, an appreciation of, and, most important, an understanding of each other's strengths.

Left: *Allium christophii* displays like fireworks at the base of a column. **Below**: A pink *Abutilon* nods in the evening light.

PLANTING MYSTERY IN THE GARDEN
[David]

Archaeology, with its adventure and mystery influenced me at a young age. I was fascinated by the early explorations of Frederick Catherwood, a nineteenth-century British archaeologist and illustrator, whose pen-and-ink drawings captured images of the ancient world in the days when photography was in its infancy. In addition to his travels on the Nile and in the deserts of Egypt, he visited the jungles of Central America with famed explorer John L. Stephens, accurately illustrating ancient monuments previously unknown and unseen by most of the world. He endured hardship and toil as he carved his way through the heat of the jungles to expose these magnificent stone ruins. With each swing of his machete in clearing the jungle trail, he was on a path of mystery and discovery.

I like to think of myself and other visitors as Catherwoods in our garden. Although George would be most unhappy if I began to wield a machete and carve out pathways in our garden "jungle," Catherwood's sense of adventure inspires my own sense of exploration. Our garden is small, yet vast with possibilities for discovery: Pushing large, leafy, overgrown plants from the path as you pause to take in what lies ahead, stepping forward into the unknown of your own urban "jungle," you can have the feeling of a grand personal adventure. You hear the sound of water but don't yet see its source. The lyrical music of a gentle dripping fountain lures you deeper into the maze of plantings and textures. For a moment you are lost in the pleasure of your own discoveries.

Such short forays as these enhance the feeling of exploration in our garden. When you include a few elements of discovery and surprise in

Preceding pages: Broad pavers in the entry court absorb heat in summer, keeping the potted tropicals warm at night, and set off gunnera and sphere sculptures. **Left**: The Lemon Mirror in full sun mysteriously reflects a darker part of the garden.

your own garden, you add the special quality of mystery. It is what turns a mundane and predictable garden saunter into a stimulating and inspiring garden adventure. By having fun, using your imagination, and not being afraid to create a little mystery, you can make your garden personal, exciting, and distinctive.

TAKING RISKS
[G e o r g e]

When we began our garden years ago, it was as sculptors who loved gardening. We did not have, and still do not have, a plan for how the place should look or what it would become in the future. We started for simple enjoyment in the act of gardening and a love of the results, of the atmosphere that it produced. We appreciated how it made us feel. From the beginning we were keenly aware of our feelings about, or our impressions of, pot arrangements, plantings in beds, placement of fountains, and uses of color. Did the area we had just changed from the previous year or newly re-made this year move us in some way? How? How did it seem to affect visitors? We gardened by just doing what worked for us, though we also wanted to know something about *how* it worked without attempting to intellectualize it too much. Plant taxonomy, soil mixtures, chemical analyses are all good and necessary, but it was a more ineffable quality that led to our style of gardening in the first place. Like a painting, it is what it is: The experience is the important thing. And, as in the process of making a painting, it is vital not to "over-paint," to over-plan the garden. We wanted to let it be as fresh and spontaneous as we could, without being in thrall to a *plan.*

Sedum morganianum (burro's tail) pours like water from a planting of bromeliads in the greenhouse.

Left: Persian shield
(*Strobilanthes*) and a variety
of coleus by the lotus pool.
Below: *Begonia* 'Freddy',
given to us by a friend more
than 25 years ago, has huge
leaves with red undersides
and delicate flowers.

With our hard-won concrete techniques, we set out to give the garden and our work what we call an "excavated look"—that is, we tried to evoke ancient cultures with the use of muted color washes for the columns, walls of earthy terra-cotta and Mediterranean blue, and over-scale plantings of large-leaved perennials and tropical-looking plants grouped in clay pots of various sizes. So, over time, and keeping our desired look in mind, we gradually made a garden that we love,

and, if reactions are any indication, that other people do too. There was a lot of trial and error, but we don't carry the burden of how our garden *should* look. Many of the things that make the garden appealing, such as some of the sculpture and smaller columns, are easily movable, the better to suit our annual desire to give the place a different look. We allow ourselves to take risks with color, so the garden has a regularly changing look that appeals to our (and our visitors') sense of entering a new garden, even though many of the elements are unchanged from the previous year.

The emphasis here is on the importance of *not* putting yourself into a box when it comes to creative decision-making. Introduce change as the core of your garden, and let go of the anxiety about what you think it ought to be. If a wall is the wrong color, change it. It's only paint. Have you felt frustrated and guilty for years over that straggly old rhodie? Throw it out and put in something more rewarding and enjoyable. The garden should be a place of celebration, whether contemplative and quiet, or buoyant and colorful, or all of these. What it shouldn't be is a source of annual conflict with your own good intuition. One morning not long ago I misread "clarity of perception" as "charity of perception." What a wonderful way to describe perceiving the world of the garden as it is. A nonjudgmental and openhearted approach is certainly the best way to act on your own creative instincts, including gardening, and it needn't preclude exercising a discerning yet compassionate eye.

One of the most successful gardens I've seen in this respect is the large woodland garden at Heronswood Nursery near Kingston, Washington. Our good friends there, Robert Jones and Dan Hinkley, commissioned us to make an archaeological ruin that resembled a

The Temple at Heronswood Nursery as seen across a boggy pool; *Petasites japonicus* var. *giganteus* leaves inspired the sculpture group at center.

fallen temple for one of the boggy and more tropical areas of the garden. We put in a 12-foot-diameter pool surrounded by seven blue Doric-style columns, each 8 feet tall. Some were connected with curved lintel planters, while some were made to look as if they had broken and fallen and been left on the site. Now the "temple" is grown around with lush tropical looking plantings: dicksonias and musas, gunneras and darmeras, and many others. It is truly beautiful and

Below: This Bocca di Veritas looks as if it might speak! **Right**: The Snakes and Grapes Fountainhead with *Solanum quitoense* covered in purple fuzz in the foreground.

how to add mystery to the garden

Use large broad-leaved plants that hang out over the path and need to be pushed aside as you wander the garden to add to the allure of what is ahead. Three favorites that grow in the most temperate zones are *Hosta* 'Sum and Substance' (perfect for shady areas), *Petasites japonicus* var. *giganteus*, and the beautiful hydrangea 'Ayesha'.

Create a garden cul-de-sac by having a pathway dead end, forcing the visitor to retrace his steps and thereby adding a little mazelike adventure to his garden wandering.

Hide a water feature in a garden bed, behind a tree, or around a bend so that you hear the sound of water before you actually see its source.

Tuck a small piece of artwork into an unexpected or less obvious place so that visitors may or may not see it on their first pass through.

Create areas that are off limits by using a simple sign, a barrier of planted containers, or a gate so that a visitor wonders what is beyond.

Include garden "rooms"—small, contemplative spaces that feel far removed from the garden as a whole and where a visitor may linger in solitude.

Left: *Epiphyllum* 'Deutsche Kaiserin'. **Right:** A path leads from shade to a sunny area, passing by *Smilacena racemosa* in flower, hostas, and a basin favored by robins.

Left: The Stalactite Man Fountainhead; Baby's Tears adorn its crown where chick-adees sometimes cling to drink drops of water. **Below**: Jewel-like *Tradescantia andersoniana* 'Blue and Gold'.

draws many visitors. Dan and Robert were open to putting in some-thing unusual and perhaps a little risky, and the result is an atmos-pheric, lovely spot in their universally acclaimed garden. A little folly can be a good thing.

Picasso said that every time he faced a blank canvas he risked every-thing. Obviously, we can't all be great masters, but the point is to be true to your dreams of a garden paradise, your own instincts and imagination.

"NATURE IS NOTHING BUT THE TRUTH.
THAT IS WHAT WE ARE TOO, IF WE SLOW DOWN,
TURN AROUND, AND ACKNOWLEDGE
OUR BONES AND ROOTS."

| CHAPTER TWO |

bones of the garden

ANCIENT BEGINNINGS
[David]

WHEN GEORGE AND I SET OUT to create our garden, there was no design. We never put anything down on paper that resembled a landscape design or a blueprint. The "bones" of our garden have been molded by spontaneity, changing visions, and a continuing desire to challenge ourselves. This framework may be influenced by a new plant purchase or by a just-finished sculpture that needs to be placed. An area of lawn might simply look out of place within the jumble of "rooms" and plantings, so we rework the grassy space. A mood swing or a more practical spatial need can alter the garden's entire layout.

There is something very satisfying about not following a plan. Each season we can approach the garden as an artist would tackle a fresh or only slightly worked canvas. The bones of our garden are built on our shared memories, passion, hard work, and lots of compromise.

In 1970, when I was a teenager, my family spent a year in a small fishing village on the island of Crete in the Aegean Sea. My father, an

Gunnera and lotus leaf sculptures nestle beneath a *Solanum aviculare* and *Canna* 'Tropicana'.

attorney, realized that his profession rarely allowed sabbaticals, so he self-imposed one, packed up his family, and took us to that mountainous, windswept island. I spent the year exploring the rugged countryside and was captured, even at a young age, by the beauty and mystery of the ancient ruins and rocky outcroppings scattered over the sage-covered hills. It was a very impressionable period of my life that, thirty-five years later, still inspires my gardening style.

Before we developed our garden on Wing Point, there was only a nondescript yellow lawn stretching from the front door to the street. Several overgrown boxwoods shielded the door to the house and gave the property its only privacy. An early-blooming rhododendron, butchered by years of bad pruning, spent its blooms in early March and was an eyesore the rest of year.

A fortuitous gift of some soot-covered bricks from a fallen chimney gave rise to the footprint of the early garden. We stacked bricks one on top of another to create the outlines of long, narrow, rectangular beds. We removed the grass from inside these beds and replaced it with a mixture of one-half good topsoil and one-half organic nutrients, usually composted cow manure ordered from our local dairy. As the garden

The original yard in 1988, left, and how it looks now, right.

began to take shape, it resembled a 3000-year-old Minoan village like those half buried in the terra-cotta–colored dirt of Crete, with overgrown walls poking up from the ground and a meandering maze of narrow passages and open grassy courtyards. Suddenly, our garden had the elements reminiscent of my childhood adventure in Greece: mystery, discovery, and a sense of ancient presence.

Using bricks to outline garden beds is an excellent way not only to incorporate and reuse found objects but also to retain the soil and contain the plants. Our brick borders are anywhere from one to three

Below: Old bricks tentatively hold back a *Euphorbia griffithii* 'Fireglow' with its promise of spectacular orange-red bracts.
Right: George at work on the capital for the Coconut Palm Column; the timer reminds him to move the sprinkler.

ancient gardens

On the tiny volcanic island of Thira, 70 miles north of Crete, there lived a highly civilized population during the second millennium before Christ. The settlement, called Akrotiri, was part of a larger community of Minoans who inhabited the island of Crete. The ancient civilization distinguished itself by building large, complex stone palaces and creating artistic works that reflected their carefree character and love of nature. The settlement was destroyed by a cataclysmic volcanic eruption some 3,500 years ago, but archaeologists have been recently uncovering magnificent painted frescoes that reflect the daily life of the island's peaceful inhabitants. Most significant are the paintings depicting their passion for gardening and nature. These partially restored wall frescoes show colorful swallows frolicking among clumps of red lilies, gazelles and monkeys in royal gardens, and small intimate fountains in courtyards. Other paintings show figures gathering saffron from crocuses and domesticated birds meandering in garden foliage. These lovely and serene depictions of early gardens highlight our timeless appreciation for nature's beauty and the human need to garden since the dawn of civilization.

Below: A fragment of the painting Crows and Daylilies (27 by 72 inches).
Right: Detail of Japanese Anemones, a set of three repeating concrete tiles.

bricks high. If all the brick courses were the same height, the beds would look too planned and calculated; creating differing heights gives them a look of ancient disrepair. The natural unevenness of the property also helped to create the impression of ruins, and we took advantage of it. Just as an archaeological site has walls that start and end with no apparent reason, the natural terrain dictates our garden borders.

As our original brick supply began to run low, we supplemented with beach stones and store-bought bricks. Over time, though, all the bricks became moss-covered and looked as if they had been there for millennia. And because they are so small and portable, we can easily change the shape, size, and orientation of a garden bed without too much labor.

VERTICALITY
[George]

Our garden is a relatively small space, and even as we created more beds we quickly found that we were running out of room for new plant specimens. How could we satisfy our plant enthusiasms while maintaining the tranquil, uncrowded feeling that we so much enjoyed? We liked to collect unusual plants with large foliage and a tropical look, particularly for the inspiration such plants provide for our sculptures, and our collection soon became large. We had laid out a good skeleton for the garden with our brick borders and with sculptures placed in strategic spots, usually functioning as fountains. We also used columns as fountains and pergolas. We usually use color washes on the columns, faded and transparent, to enhance the feeling of architectural ruins. These strong verticals suggest the remains of larger structures and, thus, create an atmosphere of the distant past combining with the present. And

Musa basjoo at the top left shelters blue *Senecio mandraliscae* on a column, while silver *Centaurea cineraria* in a raised pot overlooks *Sedum spectabile* 'Autumn Joy'.

a row of columns, large or small, can lengthen the viewer's sense of perspective and make a small space seem mysteriously larger.

Making columns is, in fact, an integral part of our work as artists. In addition to suggesting architectural remains of ancient cultures, we use them as part of our garden's bones as in the blue pergola in the entry court. We make our columns in sections, so we always have pedestals available at just about any height, and we use those in our greenhouse as plant stands and shelves to hold all of our tropical specimens during the winter.

One day we grouped a few columns together in the garden's entry court and decided to place some potted tropical specimens on their capitals. We suddenly realized this was the way to go: up! Placing plants on top of the columns gave us much-needed new areas for gardening in a small space. But it also looked great, letting us see the plants from unusual angles—a new and exciting experience. Several of the tropicals, now high off the ground on columns or pedestals, suggested the forms found in a grove of palm trees. The architectural accent from the strong verticals also appealed to our sense of drama and helped tie the existing pergolas to the rest of the garden. Of course there are as many ways to raise pots off the ground as there are people with imagination: columns, chimney flue tiles, sections of painted PVC pipe, inverted pots of all sizes, large stones, felled tree sections—the list is limitless.

The response of visitors to this vertical aspect of our garden has been intriguing. Because they find themselves seeing plants from unexpected angles—for instance, looking *up* at the underside of foliage and flowers—people tend to feel more involved in a tour of the garden. The columns and raised pots help visitors to really focus on and enjoy individual plants and structures. Instead of wondering what to make

Yellow-gold *Laburnum watereri* 'Vossii' wafts toward the cave-like mouth of a concrete sphere; *Euphorbia griffithii* 'Fireglow' at lower right.

for dinner that night, they seem to participate in the present moment more fully. It's not only the vertical arrangements that do this, of course, but when one is presented with an unavoidable and different perspective, even a small experience like touring a garden can bring about a feeling of change or excitement.

CREATING ROOMS
[David]

Early on, the small 5- by 12-foot pool that was our first structural collaboration was centered in the lawn and surrounded by bricks to tie it into the rest of the developing garden. This pool not only acted as a focal point for the garden but also evoked the wells of ancient villages. In Minoan Crete, the water source was also the community's "life-source," providing sustenance and acting as the hub for village activity and social encounters. Using our first water feature as a center, or hub, helped us align the garden beds and create the pathways and courtyards that would eventually give the garden its feeling of many rooms.

In the summer season the beds, laid out like archaeological sites, are five and six feet deep in perennials that form walls separating one part of the garden from another. This creates the "rooms," small, intimate spaces defined by the plantings as well as by architectural and hardscape features. The rooms make a small garden seem larger as you wander and discover each new space. They can hold a hidden treasure: a small water feature that you might hear before you see, a dramatic plant, a sculpture, or just a place for quiet retreat. Our entire garden is built, expanded, and changed with the use of such rooms and the serene, mysterious air they create.

Right: The pool "room," home to tropical water lilies, lotus, two fountains, and countless goldfish.
Following pages: *Kerria japonica* blossoms drift like sparks before a blue wall.

CREATING WALLS

[George]

What's interesting about how gardeners see walls is that, most of the time, they don't seem to see them at all! Even if you have designed the house or garden yourself, it's easy to overlook the walls as actual elements that can create mood and atmosphere in your garden. But if you

think of wall space—whether it's an ordinary brick wall, a rough wood fence, or an imposing stucco barrier—as a canvas available for design and color, your garden concept can change in a hurry.

Painting some kind of flat plane, such as a wall surface, with a broad sweep of accent color can make it an unforgettable sight at the end of a garden path or as you round a corner. A light complementary value behind dark leaves (such as a wall painted a light yellow-green behind a dark red plum tree) or a rich dark value behind bright leaves (such as a deep lavender-blue wall showing behind a golden catalpa) can look smashing. To spot a distant blue wall through low branches or in the raking evening light can be a magical experience in the garden. We have a friend who painted an interesting fence along the street side of his garden, pairing orange-gold fence posts with a transparent magenta wash on the wide slats, all set into the top of a low stone wall. It may sound over the top, but the effect is charming and the colors feel right at home amidst the deep evergreen trees that surround the place.

In our own garden, we have a 7- by 15-foot terra-cotta–colored wall rising behind an arrangement of column fountains. The thing that's great about this surface is that it's so easy to change whenever the inclination strikes. The wall displays an array of our mirrors, paintings, and leaf sculptures that changes fairly constantly. We generally repaint the wall every year, even if only to refresh the same color we used the year before. But I think it's more fun to change the color dramatically—for example, going from a dark shade to a light tint, or from one color to its complement, such as replacing an apricot tone with a blue-green. This forces us to look at everything on and around the wall in an entirely new way. It's amazing how different old and

The cool, moist Raintree drips in its shady pool, while a nearby mirror lures sunlight from across the garden.

wall materials

Left: A circular, blue sculpture complements the round planter filled with a ring of blue-green oxalis and grass. **Below**: Detail of the Frog and Bamboo concrete tile (19½ by 38 ½ inches).

When we set out to construct the walls of our garden, we quickly learned how time-consuming and costly real stucco walls can be. As a result we searched for an alternative that would give us the strength, stability, and rustic look of stucco but with less expense. What we discovered is known as Hardipanel, a concrete board product normally used to face houses. It's available at most large lumberyards, comes in 4- by 8-foot sheets, and is textured to look like hand-troweled stucco. We built a strong fencelike framework of treated lumber and then applied the Hardipanel to it. It's turned out to be a very reliable alternative to stucco, or to traditional fencing, for that matter. The panels, which come in a dull putty color, can be easily painted with exterior house paint to give a splash of color to the garden. And this kind of wall is an excellent surface for highlighting a plant, hanging a piece of art, or blocking an undesirable view.

familiar plants, sculptures, pots, and beds seem when a new color materializes in the space. It's like painting a room in your house a new color, and suddenly you have a refreshed perspective on the room and its furnishings.

Below: Tetrapanax and lotus leaf sculptures hover around a small sphere. **Right**: Intently placing an ivy leaf, a pair of birds enlivens our Thrush Fountain.

> "THERE IS A DEEP MYSTERY BEHIND THE
> CONSTANTLY CHANGING WORLD THAT INSPIRES
> AWE AT THE SIGHT OF SOME NATURAL OCCURRENCES—
> A STORM FRONT, A RIVER GORGE, OR A LONE TREE."

| CHAPTER THREE |

brave plantings

OVERSIZED FOLIAGE
[George]

DAVID AND I BOTH LOVE HUGE-LEAVED PLANTS that look primeval.
Sometimes we have to restrain our desire to make the garden look like
a jungle where we'd have to hack our way back to the house for break-
fast or dinner. The garden has a mythical feel: The visitor *expects* to find
charming or even shocking surprises around this or that turn. The
large leaves reinforce this feeling as they lean over a path or partially
obscure a view.

By midsummer our garden rooms are well established, with banks
of tall cannas, drifts of euphorbias, a palm sentinel in a stretch of lawn,
hydrangea walls—all punctuated with paths, open areas, sculpture, and
fountains. I like to think it is the blue pergola columns and other
pedestals that really tie the garden together, but I concede that all the
lush plantings and oversized leaves give the garden its character. Our
entry up the former drive is lined on the right with a banana *allée: Musa
basjoo* in five clumps, underplanted with restios and grasses. It sets the

Sunlight filters through the
leaves of *Canna* 'Tropicana'
like stained glass.

mood right away for the whole garden. On the left side is a large *Brugmansia* 'Charles Grimaldi' (which we dig up every fall and put in the greenhouse), two of our blue morning glory planters filled with annual color, and more *Musa basjoo*. The bananas have such great personality: They arch over the entry, making a protective yet welcoming gesture. And they get absolutely *huge*. One recent summer, our largest clump reached at least 20 feet high. Some individual leaves can be 30 inches wide and 10 feet long. (Incidentally, square sections of the leaf make terrific placemats at dinner, or you can even use them as plates at a garden party. One or two of the 10-foot leaves look wonderful down the middle of a long table.)

Another plant in the large-foliage category that must be mentioned is *Tetrapanax papyrifer* 'Steroidal Giant'. If you are in zone 8 or higher, it is a must-have for the garden for its strongly sculptural and beautiful jade-green leaves covered with silver fuzz. What a beast! The trunk reaches 12 feet high or more, and the palmate leaves, deeply cut into lobes, can be nearly 5 feet in diameter. This fabulous plant adds a distinct primordial feeling to any garden.

We created one of our herbaceous "walls" with a very tall *Canna* 'Omega'. It achieves 10 to 12 feet in height and has little, narrow, apricot flowers high at the top. But the leaves are actually the main attraction: a most beautiful glaucous blue-green and shaped like the oar of an ancient Egyptian boat, wide at the rounded base, long and pointed at the tip. It grows densely, spreading readily in all directions, a hardy and enduring beauty.

Then there's gunnera. Even the name sounds like a thud. This huge water-loving pachyderm of a plant is just that, an elephantine upspringing hulk. *Gunnera manicata* is the one we see every summer growing

The leaves of *Colocasia fontanesii* are waxy and reflect the sapphire blue of a summer day.

architectural- and sculptural-looking plants

- *Melianthus major.* Silver-green leaves with pinking-shear edges; smells like peanut butter when you crush the leaves between your fingers.

- *Inula magnifica.* This large perennial has broad, sweeping, spear-shaped leaves that can reach 5 feet in length. Insignificant clusters of yellow flowers adorn 8-foot stems in late summer.

- *Petasites japonicus* var. *giganteus.* Round, light-green leaves 24 to 36 inches in diameter.

- *Canna* 'Omega'. Twelve-foot-tall stalks with gorgeous oar-shaped leaves.

- Bananas. *Musa basjoo* is very hardy.

- *Zantedeschia aethiopica* varieties (calla lilies). Perrenial; white chalices held above dark green spearhead leaves.

- *Phyllostachys bambusoides* (giant timber bamboo). Can grow 20 to 30 feet tall.

- *Darmera peltata* (umbrella plant). "Parasols" on stems 4 to 5 feet tall.

- *Dicksonia antarctica* (Tasmanian tree fern). Risky in zone 8, but well worth it! Ours has fronds that are 10 feet long with a spread of about 15 feet across.

- *Tetrapanax papyrifer* 'Steroidal Giant'. Huge, deeply cut leaves can be 5 feet across.

Detail of a tropical-themed mirror with spiky fruit.

- *Trachycarpus wagnerianus.* A beautiful palm with neatly rounded leaves held symmetrically.

by a little stream at our friend and fellow gardener Linda Cochran's home. The dark green, palmate leaves reach 5 to 6 feet in diameter, and the plant can reach 9 feet tall. With its rough-textured surfaces and thick spiky stems, it always makes me think of Audrey the alien plant-monster in *Little Shop of Horrors*. It looks as if it could eat you while peacefully smiling away in the mud.

I'm very fond of all calla lilies for their forms, colors, and fragrance, but there is one in particular that I ran across last year in San Francisco at the Strybing Arboretum plant sale: *Zantedeschia aethiopica*

'Hercules'. In the arboretum's border, it was at least 5 feet tall with leaves more than 2 feet long and voluptuous white flowers each the size of a dinner plate. I brought a small one home, where in one season it grew into a clump $3\frac{1}{2}$ feet tall and flowered, too. It is now a pet.

Using your favorite large-leaved specimens in small spaces is great fun; it's exciting for the textures and sculptural effects they provide. Additionally, and somewhat paradoxically, they make the garden rooms and spaces feel larger, not only by screening other parts of the garden from the viewer but also by reducing our sense of our own personal scale. All this adds up to what was the delight of childhood: playful discovery and an intimate sense of the mysterious! If a garden can foster that in visitors, it truly is a place of great spirit. Children, in their innocence and openness, love gardens without having to think about it. They don't feel separate from nature—they can freely respond to a good thing when they come across it. The largess of a garden, the human influence on nature, is as much a source of delight for them as a mountain or a waterfall.

ORGANIC ARCHITECTURE
[George]

Sculpture of a tetrapanax complemented by an ominous-looking *Persicaria microcephala* 'Red Dragon'.

When I think of the architectural aspects of certain plants, the work of the Catalan architect Antonio Gaudí immediately comes to mind. I was influenced very early on by photos of his columns in the Parque Güell in Barcelona—those amazing shapes that seem to grow up out of the earth, some like great fungi, others like the trunks and roots of trees, all showing the relationship between architecture and the organic world. I was fascinated by Gaudí's vision of sculpture and

building as a transformation of natural forms. Now, in our own work, I'm interested in making structures that in themselves may not be strictly organic—like our columns—but that suggest an organic origin through their surface texture, color washes, and their placement in the garden. We like to juxtapose such columns and other sculpture against plants that in turn look sculptural or architectural to give the viewer a sense that everything grew up out of the same soil—or the same idea. When we plant a silvery blue-green *Melianthus major* near a series of Mediterranean-blue columns, the two reflect one another in color and structure. Tall columns planted close to a clump of taller bananas with their strong vertical trunks make a play on each other's forms. You begin to see common elements in plants and hardscapes that had perhaps escaped your notice before. To see a plant as a kind of architecture or sculpture, or to see architecture as an organic plantlike form, broadens our horizons in examining form, function, art, and nature. When visitors to our garden recognize this play on nature and artifice, their delight is palpable.

TROPICALS
[George]

Our painting Callas Before a Gorge achieves a trompe l'oeil effect when placed behind *Zantedeschia aethiopica* 'Green Goddess'.

Our passion for tropical places and tropical plants has profoundly influenced our gardening style. Since I'm really kind of a nut about it, when I go into a nursery or greenhouse that sells tropicals I tend to hyperventilate and dash around with a cart and an open checkbook. David has to run along behind the cart, slipping things back onto the growing tables. I could spend a fortune. But things usually work out between his budgeting and my dreams of overflowing tropical glory…

A great many of our larger-leafed plants, and much of our plant color, come from our collection of tropicals. Used either in pots or in the ground, tropicals can provide the essentials vital to good garden plantings—well-used color, structure, and texture—as well as more traditional plant choices do, and perhaps even better. So many tropicals are valuable for strong leaf color that you may not even need to consider flower color in a particular grouping. But a large violet-stemmed *Colocasia* next to *Canna* 'Tropicana', and *Crocosmia* 'Star of the East' with an *Agapanthus africanus* nearby, all grouped with a blooming *Tibouchina*, works awfully well for those who need flower color. I'm generally one of those.

It's very rewarding to have groups of tropical foliage and flowers every year in a temperate zone because of their brilliant leaf and flower color. Some of them, such as the *Musa basjoo*, we leave in the ground all year, as the stems are hardy to about 17 degrees Fahrenheit and the roots reportedly hardy to zero. Just this winter we had an unusual freeze to about 18 degrees, and most of the stalks of a large *Musa basjoo* clump survived. We like the adventure of "pushing the zone" by risking some of the more cold-tolerant tropicals, in pots or in the ground, that may be a little doubtful in our climate. If it doesn't work, if we lose some of them, well, it was fun while it lasted, and we move on to new things. Our garden is on the cool edge of USDA zone 8, where having a greenhouse or some other storage area to overwinter your tropicals is imperative if you get the tropical fever for less cold-hardy specimens. But, depending on your climate, some of the tougher potted ones may make it through the cold months outdoors on the south side of a house in a sunny area, with the protection of a cloth or tarp when a frost is forecast.

An enormous specimen of *Begonia boliviensis* sits in partial shade on a garden table.

One of the most enjoyable things about flowering tropicals is fragrance. It is an important part of garden appreciation for me and is always a consideration in purchasing or arranging plants. While I associate some tropical fragrances with certain locations, a flower's fragrance also can evoke what I think of as feeling-memories: sensations of waves on a dark shore, low clouds in high trees, sounds of birds, and so on. It's fascinating to me that fragrance calls up images and feelings rather than just the memory of the fragrance itself. The smell of 'White Butterfly' ginger does that for me more that any other. Right away I'm a young boy again, sitting on the bank of a little lake in Florida, listening to the summer-evening sounds, surrounded by a forest of ginger in bloom, with the alligators bellowing across the water. How does something so ephemeral as fragrance do that?

PORTABLE ARRANGEMENTS
[David]

Left: We place our portable, potted specimens in different spots each year according to whim. **Following pages**: A glimpse of our jungle includes from left: a lavender orchid, silver *Melianthus*, yellow *Lysimachia*, and a rather dour looking violet-stemmed taro.

Every year, in early May, we begin the ritual of bringing the potted tropicals and semi-hardy plants out of our aging greenhouse. It can take two days to empty the greenhouse of the potted plants that we had decided to keep the previous fall. Some of the largest potted plants can weigh upwards of several hundred pounds, and we always need to hire some brute strength for those days to help us with the move. Although exhausting work, the transfer from greenhouse to garden is exciting and full of energized creativity. It is the time when we begin to "paint" the garden canvas for the season.

As we haul the plants out, the majority go immediately into a shady holding area under some large fir trees, where they remain for several

David's ten favorite plants

1. Flanders Field poppy (*Papaver rhoeas*). So common, so red...but it reminds me of Greece.

2. Gunnera (*Gunnera manicata*). Its huge prehistoric-looking leaves makes this plant a living sculpture.

3. Blue agave (*Agave americana*). This tropical plant reminds me of our drives through the agave fields around Tequila, Mexico.

4. Passion vine (*Passiflora caerulea*). This fast-growing vine is very exotic looking. In a few seasons it covered the entire front of the house in a blanket of gorgeous flowers and fruit.

5. Empress tree (*Paulownia imperialis*). We cut it down to the ground every year, which produces huge leaves floating from a single trunk that still can grow to 25 feet high.

6. Abutilon (*Abutilon* 'Seashell'). I like all abutilons, but this semi-tropical one with its soft pink flowers is a stop-in-your-tracks beauty.

7. 'Patty's Plum' Oriental poppy (*Papaver orientale* 'Patty's Plum'). I am fond of Oriental poppies, while George doesn't like the fiery orange ones. The unusual deep purple color of this beauty seems to appease both of us.

8. Angel's trumpet (*Brugmansia* spp.). These semi-tropical plants have beautiful large pendulum flowers that hang down and are very fragrant at night. My favorite is *B. sanguinea* with its bright lipstick-red blooms.

9. Pomegranate (*Punica granatum*). I love pomegranates because of my memories of seeing these graceful trees in Greece. We have just begun to experiment with growing them in our garden.

10. All those plants that George wants to get rid of.

weeks. If they need to be divided or repotted, this is a good time to perform these tasks. This acclimatization is necessary or the tender winterized leaves of the plants will be burned in the sun. In the past we have brought the plants directly out into the garden to their place of seasonal honor, only to find them several days later browned and struggling. Patience, not one of my virtues, is important here. Some of the most sun-tolerant plants, like the agaves or yuccas, or those that sat in the greenhouse directly in the sunlight can go immediately out into the garden. After several weeks of partial shade we can begin to move the rest and place them throughout the garden gallery.

Coleus varieties are a favorite underplanting for pots.

The terra-cotta pots we use come in all shapes, sizes, and weights. Using only clay pots in the garden, a mandatory rule with George because of aesthetics, can be very expensive. We purchase our pots and containers (when we don't make our own concrete vessels) from nurseries, home-improvement stores, and wholesale pottery import companies. Some of the best deals can be found at the price clubs in early spring. They can be simple Italian or ornate low-fired Mexican, although the latter tend not to be frostproof. Occasionally we will wash the terra-cotta in verdigris or Little and Lewis Blue (a color about which we'll have more to say in Chapter Five) to give the pot a little more character and presence. As the pots age and weather and the painted wash begins to fade, they look centuries old, adding to the ancient air created by the sculptures and columns.

The semi-hardy and tropical potted plants that emerge from the greenhouse every spring add volume and an exotic feel to the garden. Their unique foliage can fill in an empty space or add vitality to a group of more common garden plants. Visitors walking through the gate often remark that they have left the Northwest and arrived at some foreign place. The more unusual greenhouse plants, the ones that command a special presence in the garden, earn a place of honor: We put them in individual containers and show them off as specimen plantings. So as not to crowd the primary plant, we rarely add more than one or two other plant types to a container. The wonderful taro *Colocasia* 'Black Magic' sits majestically in a pot surrounded by an underplanting of neon-yellow oxalis. This simple combination creates a stunning visual: long black stalks and broad leaves hovering above a deep cloud of yellow. Instead of crowding one planter with many types of foliage and textures, we group the containers themselves together to

Colocasia esculenta 'Black Magic' makes an ideal companion to bright, golden *Oxalis siliquosa* 'Sunset Velvet'.

some of George's favorite tropicals for pots

- *Abutilon* spp. (flowering maple). 'Seashell', 'Vesuvius', and 'Victor's Folly' are gorgeous.

- *Alocasia* spp. (elephant's-ear). Upright geen leaves of leathery texture; lovely companion plant.

- *Brugmansia* spp. (angel's trumpet). Pendent flowers are large and fragrant.

- *Ensete ventricosum* 'Maurelii' (Abyssinian red banana). Broad green leaves with red shadings.

- *Tibouchina urvilleana* (glory bush). Three-inch bright, intense violet flowers.

- *Carica xheilbornii* (mountain papaya). Large, deeply cut leaves and fruit, too.

- *Agave americana* 'Mediopicta Alba' (century plant). Variegated leaves with a white stripe down the middle.

- *Begonia boliviensis*. A tuberous begonia with clouds of comet-shaped, bright orange flowers on multiple tall stems.

- *Echeveria* spp. Succulents with rosettes of cool gray-green leaves, some 10 inches or more in diameter and beautifully overlaid or marked with pinks and deeper reds.

- *Sedum morganianum* (burro's tail). Fleshy, overlapping leaves form light silver-green "tails" that cascade like water from a tall planter or hanging basket.

- *Passiflora* (passion flower). Many tropical varieties available, and some of the hardies are spectacular and fragrant, too. We keep one potted with a jacaranda, where it clambers through the ferny leaves of the tree and blooms all summer.

A blossom of *Musa basjoo* cranes its neck in an eerily attentive manner; after flowering, the whole stem will die and be replaced by new plants.

emphasize the sculptural qualities of each plant. This way, the plants stay healthier and have plenty of space to maximize their development that season.

Additionally, planting a single specimen in a container gives us a better opportunity to group plants together based on size, foliage, texture, and color. As the plant goes through the season it will change, and if it does not look right or begins to look tired we can move it to another location and replace it with a plant better suited to that grouping. This portability gives us the spontaneity to change the look of parts of the garden. It also lets us introduce other types of potted plants and containers. A vessel of water may hold a favorite water plant such as a towering hardy *Thalia* or, floating at water level, multitudes of the butter cream–colored flowers of the miniature water lily *Nymphaea xhelvola*. Or we may have a still water vessel without any plantings, serving the sole purpose of reflecting the other plants around it. Each of these portable arrangements creates a sculptural focal point. The ease with which we can change the groupings is a constant source of playful creativity and change in the garden.

The leaves of Abyssinian red banana, left, are bold and structural, while *Begonia boliviensis*, right, relies on vivid color.

"JUST AS WE HUMANS SPRING FROM
ELEMENTS OF THE EARTH AND STARS, SO THEY
ARE INSEPARABLY PART OF US
IN OUR DAILY ROUNDS."

CHAPTER FOUR

elemental water

USING WATER FEATURES
[David]

WATER IS THE HEART OF OUR SMALL GARDEN REALM. Since ancient times, as villagers collected their daily water from a natural spring or well, water sources have served as focal points for socializing and conversing. Wells gradually became both more elaborate and more comfortable, the font of life-giving water honored with fountainheads and architectural surrounds. Water is obviously still essential to gardens today, nourishing plants and sustaining gardening habits, so it is only fitting that we, too, would want to honor this element with a beautiful pond or fountain, not just an on-and-off spigot. Adding a fountain or two can bring the heartbeat of your garden to life with its sound. A water source becomes a place to reflect, relax, and socialize. As in ancient times, it can create a sacred and honored space.

Most water features can be classified as either natural, formal, or sculptural. A natural water feature usually incorporates indigenous rocks to create a small mountain stream or spring, imitating perhaps the remnants of a glacier. It can be very effective in an urban setting,

Light playing on water's surface and in its depths is unsurpassed for beauty and mystery, while plants as diverse as English ivy, variegated hosta, and Hydrangea contrast with its ephemeral quality.

where it reinforces the tranquillity of nature. And when done properly, a natural feature looks as if it has always been there.

In contrast, formal water features are usually a linear shape—a rectangle or square—and they make no pretense about their man-made origins. Such pools make perfect reflective surfaces when still and are ideal for water gardening. If you choose, you can create water movement with a fountain, perhaps a simple water jet bubbling right at the surface or a fountainhead spilling water from one end of the pool.

Sculptural water features can encompass a wide selection of themes, materials, and sizes, which gives you great flexibility in choosing an appropriate feature for a particular spot in your garden. Usually self-contained, with a recirculating pump and a water basin, a sculptural fountain is easy to set up and requires nothing more than a level surface and electricity. There are many designs on the market, from mass-produced to one-of-a-kind originals. They are usually made of concrete, polyresins, or metal. You are limited only by your space, your design aesthetics, and the cost of the material you choose.

There are about fourteen different fountains and pools in our garden, all of them one-of-a-kind sculptural and semiformal. They change in number from year to year with the introduction of new sculptures and other features. And all but one rely on submersible recirculating pumps, which conserve water and require minimal maintenance. As you wander the garden you are, surprisingly, not overwhelmed by the sound of water or the presence of so many features. The subtle, lyrical water sounds intermingle with the sounds of birds, rustling leaves, and the occasional plane flying overhead. We pay careful attention to honoring the surroundings and space where a water feature is placed. Too much water noise can overwhelm the listener and create the opposite

Preceding pages: Pair *Carex elata* 'Aurea' with the brush strokes of *Phalaris* 'Gardeners' Garters' for sheer elegance. **Left:** Blue *Senecio* looks like a fretwork screen over languid goldfish.

of a soothing, reflective effect. Once, many years ago, we were invited to the home of acquaintances to see a newly installed water feature. They had designed a large cascading rockery right outside their front door, walled in on either side by the wings of the house. With the flip of a switch, huge volumes of water came cascading down the rocks into a small pool at the bottom. The noise was deafening, and all we could do was smile, since anything we said would have been drowned out. It made me anxious and irritable for the rest of the day. It also helped us coin the phrase "Niagara Syndrome" for those installations that are too big, too noisy, and way out of scale for the location. Unless, for instance, you are trying to block out the noise of a nearby highway, the sound of water should be an accompaniment to the natural sounds of the garden.

STILLNESS, REFLECTION, VESSELS, AND FOUNTAINS
[George]

Surely, gardening is one activity that helps restore our connection with nature. And one of its most important aspects is the quality of contemplative thinking born out of being an attentive gardener. If we will it, anything can hold our attention, yet some things, because of their innate qualities, more readily become a mirror for revelation. Water is one of those things. Still water, with its surface images and its depths, draws viewers into the depth and vitality of their own imaginations. Moving water, on the other hand, often suggests our own restlessness, as it always seeks its level, its place of rest. As does watching fire, observing water slows down thinking and inspires fascination—a letting-go of the daily flurry of thoughts, a relinquishing of the schedule-oriented

The clamshell fountainhead of this Etruscan feature sprouts water Forget-me-not (*Myosotis palustris*).

balancing a pond's ecosystem

Most ponds can be organically balanced without the use of mechanical filters. The right combination of plants, animals, and water movement can keep the pond healthy and algae-free. Oxygenating plants that live and grow fully submerged, such as *Elodea* or *Vallisneria*, compete with the algae for the nutrients. Because the oxygenators are a more advanced form of plant, they usually win. Putting in a good number of these plants soon after you first fill your pond with water will help suppress an algae bloom. The second group of beneficial plants are those whose leaves float on the surface, such as the water lily, lotus, and the delicate water fern *Azolla*. A good rule of thumb is to have 65 percent of your water surface covered with these plants. Another key ingredient of a healthy pond is animal life. Small feeder goldfish will control the mosquito larvae, and tadpoles and snails will eat the decomposing organic material and algae off the sides and bottom of the pool. The last component is some form of water movement, usually supplied by a submersible pump. This keeps the water aerated and oxygenated, a benefit for both plants and animals.

Left: *Nymphaea* 'Colorata'.
Right: A tiny frog camouflaged on a ginger leaf.

mind and a lighting-up of the contemplative mind, a condition that can teach us a lot about ourselves.

Some of the loveliest and most captivating elements in our garden are the vessels of water placed singly or grouped about the rooms and beside paths. Those in the sun forever reflect the changing sky; an arrangement of three of them at different heights harbors water lilies as well. Water vessels in shady spots mirror the sun through the trees, and usually have some fallen leaves floating on the surface. All of these things can inspire you to slow down and take time to observe something of beauty.

When a garden area itself is comfortable for sitting in or strolling through, a water surface inevitably draws attention and underscores that appeal. If it is rushing water, a musical fountain, or merely water moving lazily in its container, people will be taken in by the sounds and the play of light on its surface. A still, mirrorlike vessel, though, if it is large enough—say three or four feet in diameter—and dark in color can invoke imagination: a sudden flight of fantasy or a move into the depths of self-exploration. Either of these can lead to creative inspiration. J. R. R. Tolkien used with powerful effect the image of a large standing basin of water for the elf-queen Galadriel's revelatory mirror in *The Lord of the Rings*. A few years ago, David and I created a sculpture we call the Water-mirror. It is in the architectural form of a morning glory, four feet across at the top with a four-foot deep basin and a four-foot high pedestal. The inside is dark blue-black so that the water surface is highly reflective. We are continually amazed at how strongly people are drawn to that sculpture. They stand beside it, put their hands on the surface of the water, float leaves and flowers like offerings, and stay there for quite a while just gazing into the dark water and its reflections. Their

A favorite haunt of small birds, the Gunnera Leaf Fountain drips near a yellow water lily, each form echoing the other.

how to make a single-drop fountain

Simply connect a length of ¼-inch flexible copper tubing to the ¼-inch opening of a small saddle valve affixed to a faucet not far from your fountain location. The roll of tubing and the valve are standard, available at any hardware or home

improvement store, and easy to install. Then set the tube into a shallow furrow dug into the ground from the faucet to the fountain location. In our garden, we then ran the tube up the back of an old ivy-covered fir tree, tacked it to the top of an over-hanging branch using U-shaped brads, and cut it off above the exact center of a vessel resting ten feet below in a bed of *Hosta sieboldiana*. The copper tube is unnoticeable under the ivy leaves, and the end of the tube, projecting only about 2 inches out from the branch, looks like another twig to visitors standing below. Turn faucet on—just bare-ly. It will take some adjusting to get the single-drop flow. This is a very simple project that elicits big responses!

This organic-looking basin collects single drops falling from an unseen source ten feet above.

breathing seems to become quieter and deeper. Eventually, they move on to other areas of the garden, but their whole demeanor has changed: more relaxed, more receptive, more open. That something so simple should have such an effect says a lot about people's needs and the importance of water as a garden point of interest.

In our experience, certain kinds of water sounds are more pleasant than others. A big waterfall is fine at a well-judged distance. But close to the house, less volume can be more effective. We find that dripping water in lesser volumes is much more conducive to relaxation and con versation. Except at places like Tivoli Gardens outside of Rome, where there are hundreds of fountains, a single stream of squirting water is irritating in about five minutes. A much more musical sound is that of drops falling into a body of water. The higher a fountain source is above a pool, the louder the sound will generally be. Likewise, if the volume of water overflowing a dripping column, for instance, is quite low, the sounds of individual drops can be distinguished and the effect is also delightfully musical. A greater volume of water from a similar fountain creates a somewhat louder and faster dripping sound, which can generate a higher energy in the space nearby. It depends on what you want to do in a particular area, but we have found that most people enjoy the quieter and more musical sound of slow dripping. We even made a fountain with successive single drops falling from a high overhanging branch into a basin: one drop about every three or four seconds seems to keep people hypnotized, not only because of the rhythmical sound but also because each drop makes expanding rings that reverberate from the vessel's edge just as another drop falls. Because of the light at certain times of the day, the falling drops are sometimes invisible, so that visitors stand perplexed looking at the basin trying to

find the source of what's happening at the water's surface.

A rushing sound, while also calming, has a freshening effect. We have a small vessel, a jardinière, with a copper tube inside rising up to about a half-inch below the water surface. It makes a light rushing "shhhh" that is very pleasant, and it has the advantage of not splashing much at all. The overflow, running down the outside of the jardinière into a pool, aerates the water nicely—a benefit for the fish. And the low splash-out factor is good for small pools, which are typically sited in small spaces and viewed close up.

There are many types of water-jets out there for the fountain maker. But it's important to choose those that are least obtrusive (they can be big and ugly) and make a satisfying sound. Sometimes the simple homemade ones, like the "rusher" mentioned above, work the best; and often your own imagination will create something more rewarding than any store-bought plastic fountainhead (though it must be said that the plastic ones are fairly inexpensive). The bronze jets are usually quite expensive, but are much better looking and effective: The water patterns available are more varied, and the jets last a lifetime. Both plastic and bronze fountainheads and jets, along with concrete fountainheads, can be readily found on the Internet, as well as at most large garden centers. Just be careful, as there's an awful lot of junk out there that nobody should have in the garden. Treacly concrete spaniels with pansy baskets and the urinating *putti*—beware!

Nothing is quite as mysterious as a deep dark pool of water. It brings up all sorts of thoughts and feelings. We have a small pool, about five feet by twelve feet. A stone bridge, comfortable to walk on, spans its width. The water is dark and, although it's only two feet deep, seems bottomless, with just a few water-lily leaves floating under the

Preceding pages: Water wells up in the center of the Water Mirror, gently moving the glass float—a hypnotic effect. **Right**: The blue Foxglove sculpture (40 inches high) is another single-drop fountain.

overhanging bananas and tree ferns, and a pair of two-foot-long koi who have lived there for about ten years. Lovely. But you never know what people bring with them to your garden. Once a very tall and masculine man was standing on the bridge, leaning over and gazing into the depths of the water. For some reason, one of the normally shy fish chose that moment to leap about a foot out of the water right in front of him. The poor guy did an absolute tarantella and couldn't get off that bridge fast enough. I had to go into the house to laugh. Well, perhaps that isn't a fair example of a person bringing something with him. But it may be a good example of how people invest garden pools with a deeply mysterious quality. It's only natural—water is timelessly metaphorical.

WATER GARDENING
[David]

Many books are available on planning, constructing, and maintaining a water garden. It is not our intention to try to reiterate all the information that's out there. But over the years, we have learned some of the basic principles of a successful water garden, whether it is a large, well-planted natural pool or a small vessel filled with a single plant. Knowing these fundamentals will give you the confidence to experiment and be creative; then sit back and enjoy the beauty, sounds, and all the nature that a water feature attracts.

A footbridge crosses a rectangular lily pond; a pink geranium ranges in the foreground.

Location, location, location. This is probably the single most important decision to make when you contemplate adding a pond or similar water feature to your garden. First of all, choose a spot where you will be able to enjoy the pond. It can be near a patio, a walkway, or

creating a jardinière fountain

This easy-to-make fountain is both beautiful and, through the choice of vessel, expressive of your individual style. Find a glazed or earthenware jardinière that you like at a local nursery or an Oriental import store. Drill a ½-inch hole in the middle of the bottom of the vessel. (They will sometimes do this for you at the store.) Set the jardinière upright on some bricks or blocks to raise the bottom a few inches off the ground. Insert a straight ½-inch copper tube down through the hole until the bottom of the tube rests on the ground. The top end of the tube should be about an inch below the rim of the jardinière. Making sure the copper tube is vertical, fill the bottom of the jardinière with mixed concrete or mortar to a depth of two to three inches. Let this set up overnight. Now place the jardinière in your pool, setting it on bricks or stones so that its base sits just at the surface of the water in the pool. Connect the tube to a submersible pump within the pool using a length of vinyl fountain tubing (available at hardware or garden centers). Plug the pump into your electrical source and enjoy.

An antique Thai jardinière acts as a pleasant "gusher".

some other place in the garden that you frequent. Find a location where you will feel relaxed sitting and contemplating the water and its ambience. The site should be a sunny one, especially if you are planning to add water lilies. Make sure you can get electricity to the site so that you can add a fountain pump or lighting if you choose to do so. To avoid endless cleaning and unnecessary silt buildup, look for a space free of overhanging trees or plants that might drop organic material into the water. Avoiding the proximity of trees also will help when you are excavating the soil because you won't have large tree roots to contend with. Sometimes, though, you won't be able to avoid siting the pool near a tree. Don't let that stop you from enjoying water in your garden. You can construct the pool above ground. And the occasional pool cleaning will be a small sacrifice in exchange for the pleasure of having a pond.

Each time we visit clients to consult about pond locations, we are presented with a unique set of parameters for the site. But there is one rule George repeats over and over: Make the pond as big as you can in the space you have. Water gardening becomes addictive. It is low-maintenance, and with the availability of plants that are both beautiful and exciting, the pond will quickly become the heart of your garden. The most frequent mistake people make is planning their pond too small. If you think it is big enough, I promise you, it's not. As water plants develop, they can outgrow the available space of most water gardens in a single season, keeping you from adding other exciting varieties the next year. What looks adequate on paper may look too small once it's in the ground. It may help to take a garden hose and lay out an outline of the pond. Remember that increasing the size of the pond will be much more difficult after it is built.

Once you have determined the location and size, it's time to decide what type of construction: concrete or liner. Concrete pools—which I recommend you have installed only by a professional contractor because of the technical and physical demands of the installation—are beautiful, permanent, and expensive. Pools that are lined with a rubber EPDM 45-millimeter reservoir liner, available at most nurseries, are much less expensive than concrete pools. The homeowner can install them, but they don't quite have that "professional" look. Your decision will be based on expense, location, and the type of pool design, either formal or natural. It will also depend on how much you want to participate in the actual construction of your pool.

Water gardens do not have to be large sprawling ponds. Some of the most effective installations are simple basins filled with water that hold a favorite plant or two. One of our sculptures, the Morning Glory, is a blue-washed blossom-shaped vessel with a beautiful miniature water lily, *Nymphaea xhelvola*, floating on its surface. In midsummer there can be as many as 25 tiny yellow-cream water lilies dotting the water. It is simple, yet one of the most charming sights in our garden.

Any watertight container, pot, or vessel can be used to make a water garden. We like to group water pots together, in much the same way as we group potted plants, to create a variety of water surface heights and planting textures. Some of the vessels may have submersible pumps that gently move the water, while others may be perfectly still. Each reflects the light differently, and each changes during the course of the day with the movement of the sun. One of our favorite water vessels is a large concrete sphere with an opening that makes it look like a hatched prehistoric dinosaur egg. The outside of this hand-formed vessel is washed in a color of verdigris over terra-cotta, and the inside is a dark

Lotus 'Mrs. Perry D. Slocum', the leaves of which are every bit the equal of the blossom; *Begonia foliosa* is entangled in its center.

George's selected ornamental water plants

- *Typha minima* (dwarf cattail). A charming, hardy diminutive for containers.

- *Cyperus papyrus* (Egyptian papyrus). A tall and graceful tropical.

- All tropical and hardy water lilies. I particularly love 'Texas Dawn', a hardy with large butter-yellow flowers, and 'Colorata', a tropical with fragrant blue flowers.

- 'White Butterfly' ginger (*Hedychium coronarium* 'White Butterfly'). A fragrant tropical.

- *Nelumbo* spp. (lotus). There are miniature varieties that do well in pots; hardy.

- *Nymphaea xhelvola*. A miniature hardy water lily with pale-yellow flowers.

- *Thalia dealbata* (alligator flag). Stately long leaves on tall stems; hardy.

- Cannas. Many will grow in water and are hardy.

- *Zantedeschia aethiopica* (calla lily). Varieties for bog or poolside; hardy in pots, too.

- *Iris ensata* (Japanese iris). A lovely variegated form with white-striped leaves and lavender-blue flowers; hardy.

Left: We love the painterly quality of this grass 'Bowles Golden'—bright sweeps over dark water. **Right**: From top left, pink variegated bougainvillea, *Colocasia* 'Black Princess', lotuses, and bright green Baby's Tears covering a fountain.

violet. Because it is tilted toward the sun, the light bounces around its dark interior and creates a wonderful show. A gentle water movement stirred by a small internal pump gives the sculpture a life when the sun is not shining into it.

Once you have decided on a water feature, the last important element is balancing the ecology of the water. A combination of plants, fish, and water movement generated by a submersible pump will help keep the pool clean, healthy, and free of perennial algae growth. You can use filters, but they can be expensive and noisy; we prefer the organic method of stabilizing a pond. Small goldfish can be put into even the smallest water feature to help control the mosquito larvae. (Although the goldfish will survive just about any climate, it's best to think of them as "annuals" and not get too emotionally attached to them.) Once the ecosystem is in balance, the water will take on a light tea-colored tone as organic material begins to naturally decay, and you will know that you have a healthy pond.

The Sphere, or "dinosaur egg," with a frosty glass float eddying in lazy circles; behind is *Hydrangea* 'Ayesha', a favorite.

"SO MANY THINGS IN THE
ARTISTIC ACTIVITY OF GARDENING CALL
UP THE KIND OF CONTEMPLATIVE THINKING
NECESSARY TO HEALTHFUL LIVING."

| CHAPTER FIVE |

art and sculpture

SCULPTURE IN THE GARDEN
[D a v i d]

SINCE ANCIENT TIMES, when the Greeks and Romans adorned their garden walls with painted frescoes and their courtyards with fountains, we have embellished gardens with our personal taste in art. The garden itself is a living work of art. It is a result of creativity and style, shaped by the maker's imagination and courage to take chances. It seems only fitting, then, to want to introduce artwork—whether we purchase, make, or find it—into this dynamic living canvas.

Even the simplest piece of artwork can draw attention to a forgotten part of the garden or highlight a well-traveled area. The change of material, from soft and leafy to hard and man-made, brings variety and a momentary challenge to our senses. A concrete-framed mirror placed in a shadowy area pulls light to an otherwise dim spot; we look twice to see whether it is a reflection or a window we are looking through. Sculpture and artwork also provide a perfect means to introduce color into the garden. A brightly colored sculptural element lures the eye across the garden to a distant point, inviting

Our Leafbeard Planter with an ice plant (*Delosperma*) and burro's tail (*Sedum morganianum*).

exploration. For example, we have an oversized concrete sculpture of a pomegranate washed in deep reds and oranges. We will often place this portable sculpture in one remote corner of the garden or another, where it pops out from nearly every angle. Alternatively, the bright lime-green colors of our concrete gunnera leaves float above the more earthy colors of the garden, a more organic integration of the natural and the man-made. Take care not to overwhelm the garden with the size of your artwork. As with the sound of water from a fountain, less is more. The results will be just as striking, but the artwork won't take away from the natural beauty your garden already projects.

An intuitive gardener can add art and ornamentation to a garden easily and spontaneously: The choice and placement of artwork comes as naturally as working in the garden itself. For many of us, though, the process is one of trial and error. We find a piece of art or sculpture we like and then struggle to find a prominent place for it. Or we have a location that we think is perfect and we begin our search for that *perfect* piece of art. I believe both approaches are wrong and not in sync with the natural rhythm of the garden. It's fine to acquire an object of art that you like and want to place in the garden; but let the garden help you come to a decision on where it belongs. Don't reveal everything at once. Put the sculpture or artwork off center, obscured by a plant, or hidden in a less-traveled part of the garden, where it will create a revelation about you and your garden. It's okay to downplay the position of the artwork—and by doing so you will foster a more natural union between the plants and the art.

Collecting artwork should take a lifetime. Sometimes a spot in the garden speaks out to be filled with a plant or piece of art. The tendency

A gunnera sculpture washed with lime green glows amid darker grasses and taro.

is to run out to the local nursery or gallery for something, anything, to fill the hole. I do it all the time. Archaeologists excavating heavily decorated Greek pottery had a term for this: *horror vacui,* "fear of empty places." A client once purchased one of our mirrors for a house in Hawaii. She said she had been looking for years for the right piece to fill this one spot and that until that day's purchase it had remained empty. I admired the slow and deliberate process she had taken. Acquiring and placing artwork, whether in the garden or the home, is more natural and successful when we are not rushed by our fear of the empty space or need for instant gratification. Take time with your search and your decision, living with the empty space until you and the garden find the perfect piece.

THE LANGUAGE OF COLOR
[George]

Color conveys feeling so readily that we use it as garden creators, consciously or not, to disclose our moods at any seasonal moment. Of course, the first things we think about in making a garden are the plant materials and the color relationships among them. But, as any landscape designer or architect will tell you, among the first things that we should be considering is the hardscapes: the structure, walls, pergolas, pools, fountains, sculpture, and so on that give the garden its base, its character, its bones. And these structures can all be a powerful generative force behind the moods and feelings at work in your garden, not only through their shapes and their architectural or sculptural presence but also—and especially—through the colors you decide to give them.

Left: A corner of a blue Doric arbor frames an early-season selection of potted specimens. **Following pages**: The Raintree features Baby's Tears and Hart's Tongue ferns; a bas-relief triptych of citrus and leaves hangs in the background.

In our garden we have a pergola of seven eight-foot-high Doric-type columns of our own design. They were cast from a muted terra-cotta–colored concrete and then washed with a beautiful medium-intensity blue that we have come paternally to call Little and Lewis Blue. (We use this particular color a great deal, as we have discovered that every single plant and flower in the garden likes it.) The wooden crosspieces on the capitals of the columns were painted the color of aged copper roofs— a fairly intense verdigris. The combination of the blue and green can be seen from all over the garden. It makes the pergola playful and elegant, grand and welcoming, all at once and sets the mood for the whole place. Then, too, the placement of sculpture, such as a 30-inch-diameter red pomegranate on a little blue pedestal at the end of a path, adds tremendously to the effect. But the columns are magical to me in this regard. While their strong verticals lend various degrees of stateliness, their colors do impart a sense of playfulness, and this, in concert with big architectural plants, really does give one the feeling of wandering, like Alice, in a wonderland. Granted, David and I don't shy away from the whimsical, but at the same time, we don't want to get sentimental with hardscapes or plantings, so we use unexpected colors, plants, and sculpture in unusual places to surprise and even shock.

Experience has shown us to think not only about the colors we like but also about what moods they create in us and how each of those moods works in the garden. Any unusual use of color involves taking a risk. But, as we keep emphasizing, that is what creativity is all about and what makes gardening fun and keeps your process from becoming stale. Color provides a perfect avenue for enjoyable risk-taking! People perceive color emotionally, not just visually; it speaks a language that expresses your feeling life as it develops through your discoveries in the

A dusky agave lurks beneath a light-hearted *Brugmansia* where the arbor's crosspieces meet.

little and lewis blue

Some of the first blooms up in spring in our garden are the flowers of *Brunnera* 'Jack Frost', bright forget-me-not lavender-blue. We have seen this color a lot on weathered buildings in Mexico and have come to claim it as our own. We can't really explain why we love this color as much as we do—perhaps it is simply so reminiscent of places we love. But the fact is that it just looks wonderful anywhere in the garden—in plants, architectural elements, or sculpture. Determined to replicate this color for our art, we spent hours in the studio, blending and concocting, until we created a color that matched the blue of our travel memories and approached the hue of the brunnera flower. Our pergola is this blue; we painted a whole wall in this color. Somehow, we never tire of it. It is a relaxing blue, of medium intensity, not a cold or pale shade as blues often are. It is intriguing, too, because it changes with the light throughout the day: Shadows that fall on it are deep lavender, while spots of light touch down as bright blue. Sometimes, in the evening, when the painted wall blends into the twilight, it looks as if you could put your hand right through it. And the color has a magical quality: It brings the sky down to earth. We call it Little and Lewis Blue with a smile because we use it so much and can't seem to sculpt or garden without its showing up somewhere.

Left: A selection of hosta sculptures illustrates our unrestricted use of color. **Right**: The Raven Fountain and a rheum leaf sculpture both utilize Little and Lewis Blue.

garden. It's a very personal thing, and no one can tell you what is right or wrong. Let color teach you: Only experience and trial and error can show you what works or doesn't in your own garden.

The uses of color in gardening are often about emotion. Whether excitement or calmness, such a mood is achieved in part by color complements, shades, and tints. Here are some things we've learned over the years about using each.

The complement of a color is its opposite on the color wheel. For instance, the complement of blue is orange, of red is green, of yellow is violet. Complements closely juxtaposed usually generate energy, vibration, and tension. By mixing complements together, however, you also can mute a color—just as in painting, a very intense orange may need a little blue mixed into it or placed nearby to quiet it down, so to speak. The same complement principles apply in gardening. We have a towering *Eucalyptus glaucescens* over a large clump of *Crocosmia* 'Lucifer': silver blue-green over brilliant red-orange. They make each other vibrate, yet also settle into each other and beautifully blend in the space. A diminutive lime-green *Oxalis vulcanicola* underplanting *Colocasia* 'Black Magic' with its dark red-black leaves has caught the eye of everyone who visits our garden.

Plants usually seen in borders can be much more dramatic as potted color accents, like this *Crocosmia* 'Star of the East'; an *Agapanthus africanus* is at lower left.

Shades and tints are pretty obvious: A shade is a color darkened with black, thereby darkening its mood, and a tint is a color lightened with white, thereby lightening its mood. So, pink is a tint of red, while deep burgundy is one of its shades. Imagine a planting of Oriental poppies: a drift of blossoms grading from pale pink through apricot, red, and the dusky dark wine of the cultivar 'Patty's Plum'. The flowers relate in color and texture above their fuzzy green leaves, a delightful progression that draws the eye along. The possibilities are numberless.

ARTFULNESS AND CEREMONY
[George]

A wise friend once said to me, "We garden because we remember Paradise." I think we must all be aware of some of the wonderful myths of the Garden of Eden—so it seems proper to me here that we might ask ourselves what the Paradise garden is. If we think of it in terms of a heavenly place in the afterlife, a landscape of ease and beauty, then perhaps we look at our own gardens as lovely reflections of that image. If we feel that Paradise is a state of mind and heart in which there is no longer a separation from the object of our souls' longing for wholeness, then we have surely begun a quest for the nature of wholeness. I believe that gardening is a ritual activity, a sacred bonding, in this sense—like a marriage between your garden and self, which requires a renewal of your vows. In the garden, nature is malleable yet great; truthful yet changing and mysterious; sweet as the bees yet mighty as desire; melancholy and joyful all at once, the embodiment of wholeness. So a daily acknowledgment of our relatedness to the elemental realms of the garden, some ritual gesture in which we might mindfully and physically renew our connection to nature, would be helpful. A small offering, a leaf on a stone or a flower in a vessel of water, is little enough, yet great enough to recognize our participation in the garden and the day to come.

Almost any garden activity can become a ritual for reconnecting ourselves with nature: Clean away the dust and small debris from the reflective eye of a water vessel; water the potted plants with the understanding that you give them life; play calming music lightly in the garden, for the plants as much as for yourself; sit down and thoroughly appreciate it all. Just feeding the fish with an awareness of a connection

Preceding pages: One of our favorite arrangements in the garden takes advantage of two portable elements, the Pomegranate and a variegated fuchsia.
Right: A *Tetrapanax* leaf appears more artful after the first frost.

with them through the activity—that's all it takes to enliven one's feeling for the day. The vow is the thing, the personal vow for awareness, for simple consideration for the existence of other beings: the vow to be attentive. That's what the garden calls for, what it wants from us in return for having given us so much so naturally.

some favorite plants for color

- *Catalpa bignonioides* 'Aurea' (golden catalpa). Large, heart-shaped, bright yellow-green leaves that light up any corner of the garden. Hardy, a large tree.

- *Rosa glauca*. Gunmetal blue-gray foliage; small, single pink flowers. A wonderful companion to *Cotinus coggygria purpureus* (purple smoke tree).

- *Eucalyptus glaucescens*. A tall and airy tree whose leaves, branches, and trunk stay silver-blue year-round.

- *Crocosmia* 'Lucifer'. Slender, 60-inch-tall leaves with sprays of fire-engine-red flowers. Makes a great sprawling clump.

- Hydrangeas. We like all of them! Heavy mops or lacecaps from white through blue, red, and pink. The hortensias look like big-bosomed dowagers holding court in a corner of the garden, while the lacecaps are delicate and elegant.

- *Cupressus cashmeriana*. A truly beautiful cypress with pendulous branches whose leaves are glaucous, with yellow-green tips.

- *Olea europaea* ssp. *cuspidata* (olive). A self-fertile variety with small, deep purple fruit; hardy to zone 8.

- *Euphorbia griffithii* 'Fireglow'. A fabulous perennial for late spring with its pink-and-orange emerging foliage and orange-red flower bracts that radiate hot color.

Crocosmia 'Lucifer' is a dynamic presence beneath a lavender-pink *Lythrum* and a towering, silvery *Eucalyptus glaucescens*.

When this attentiveness is combined with an eye for gardening, the garden becomes artful. Humans have an impulse for the beautiful, a desire for it. We strive to make our gardens lovely in some way: tender, strong, striking, lyrical. And since the perception of beauty develops as we go along, like a talent long practiced, we become more and more attuned to and confident in the garden as our own personal expression

of artfulness. This artfulness appears in the garden itself or in concert with sculpture and hardscapes. In any case, the more attentive we are to the garden and to nature, the more we discover about ourselves and the more we have to give back to the garden creatively. Gardening is a celebration of joyful, artful collaboration.

> Beloved, gaze in thine own heart,
> The holy tree is growing there;
> From joy the holy branches start,
> And all the trembling flowers they bear.
> The changing colours of its fruit
> Have dowered the stars with merry light;
> The surety of its hidden root
> Has planted quiet in the night;
> The shaking of its leafy head
> Has given the waves their melody,
> And made my lips and music wed,
> Murmuring a wizard song for thee.

> —from *The Two Trees* BY W. B. YEATS

Influenced by the colors of adjacent *Persicaria* 'Painter's Palette', a taro leaf sculpture rests on a bench.

| CHAPTER SIX |

time and rhythm

MUSIC AND LIGHT
[George]

I LOVE THE RHYTHMS of the passing light. One of the most beautiful and pleasurable things about being in a garden is noticing how light, at any time of the day or night, fills the place with vitality, with something that seems like consciousness. Well, light in its metaphorical sense *is* consciousness. It transforms darkness; it allows us to understand our surroundings; it gives us the capacity to move more freely. We learn as a result of its presence—just as when human consciousness is shone on the world. So when light moves across the face of a garden, changing our perceptions of things by the minute, it inspires us to embrace innovation. It inspires us to be present to the rhythms of the changing world. Not to mention the sheer gorgeousness of light on the surface of things.

One of the most evocative visuals in the garden comes when light filters down through tall trees and falls into dark water, making pools of muted light on the bottom. It's like glimpsing the underworld: An occasional fish swims through a shaft of light like a ghostly undine;

Autumn's level light illuminates the gnarled branches of a Japanese maple planted nearly forty years ago.

aquatic grasses undulate in slow motion; leaves in partial states of decay are visible on the bottom. It might be a dream.

Light coming through leaves and glancing across walls or sculptural elements is so lovely that you should try to plan for it. As the sun passes over our garden, arcing directly overhead, the shadowy patterns lengthen from spots to long fingers moving down the face of a wall. The effects are wonderful and different each time you look during the course of the day. Shadows also fall beautifully over the cylindrical shapes of columns and sculpture. Any architectural surface or color with leaf and branch patterns becomes a virtual tapestry—something to think about when planning a garden.

Some of the most intriguing light effects can occur with mirrors. Throughout the garden we have placed mirror-panels—bas-relief sculptures with mirrors worked into the design. When one of these is hung in a shady area, on a wall or maybe under a tree, it seems to draw the light from the sunnier parts of the garden. I can be standing in an area fifty feet away from the shaded mirror, yet it will be the mirror I see, like a window into another sunlit garden. Somehow the mirror really seems to collect light within itself. On the other hand, if it is hung in a well-lit spot, the mirror in the sculpture most often looks darker. A mysterious phenomenon with which I can happily live!

Just as we sense the rhythms in the movement of day and night across our gardens, we can surely be aware of the underlying rhythmical patterns of the flora and fauna that make up the tangible life of the garden. There is a musicality in the forms and rhythms of the plant world that seems to echo the musical sounds of birds. I swear that the new rising fronds of the Tasmanian tree fern by the front pond even look like musical notations. They sometimes seem to respond by their

The Solar Disc sculpture collects a pool of afternoon light beside an *Agave americana* 'Mediopicta Alba'; the purple-blue flowers behind are *Geranium palmatum*.

unfurling to the singing of birds in spring. I realize what kind of trouble this statement will get me into with most gardeners; I might as well say that the tulips' rising color responds to the birds as well, a fantastic idea. But even a fantasy may become a work of art; in fact, most artistic endeavors begin as fantasy. The garden *is* musical in its rhythms and constant changes. Anyone who has seen a time-lapse film of plants growing and blooming will be aware of that. If we attune ourselves to these musical subtleties that are usually hidden from our own racing mentality, we might encounter something miraculous.

Garden sounds really are symphonic: Drops of water falling from various heights into a pool are among the most musical sounds in the world. Claude Debussy knew this: His "Reflections in the Water" is a case in point. The separate sounds made by various leafy trees in the wind; branches rattling against one another; hissing of grasses; percussion of reeds; delightful rhythm of footsteps crunching gravel; a light rushing of water, punctuated by a splashing fish; the buzz of a hummingbird and the songs of other birds—all music to the gardener, all rhythm of the seasons. How marvelous.

AT SEASON'S END
[David]

When the cool, moist marine air greets us every day and the sun begins to sink lower on the horizon, casting cold shadows through the towering pine sentinels on our property, it signals the end of another growing season. I accept the fate of the season's demise without too much disappointment, since garden maintenance can be a round of endless chores. In fact, by mid-October I am ready to put the garden to rest for

Right: By means of color and texture, much of the garden ages gracefully with the passing season.
Following pages: The studio gate opens to reveal finished sculptures waiting to be shipped; there is often a sense of melancholy in seeing sculptures go.

the season and let humans and plants alike take a break from the summer's burst of energy.

On the first of November we begin to decide which potted tropicals we will winter over in the limited space of the heated greenhouse. It is a difficult decision. Some of the tropicals have doubled their size during the summer, and we undoubtedly have been adding new varieties and transplanting others into larger vessels. For the most part I leave the plant culling to George. In fact, I prefer not to look. Those plants that make the cut are dragged into the greenhouse and carefully placed in the 18- by 24-foot structure by height, light preference, and just how

A Satyr's head punctuated by a little elf of a flower, *Abutilon* 'Sunset'.

much more energy we have to drag those heavy pots. The process can take two full days. A large propane heater keeps the temperature at a steady 58 degrees Fahrenheit. This is a compromise between the high cost of propane (and my wish to keep the greenhouse just above freezing) and George's desire to feel as though he is in Puerto Vallarta. This temperature does not encourage new growth but comfortably maintains the plants till the next summer. Fans keep the air circulating, and a few hanging yellow sticky cards keeps the whitefly under control. The potted tropicals that did not make it into the warmth and winter safety of the greenhouse are grouped in a sheltered spot outside of the studio. This concession to my angst about getting rid of *any* plant allows these poor outcasts to try to winter over on their own. Sometimes, in a mild winter, one or two out of six or so will make it through, and I will give these survivors a place of honor in the next season of the garden.

Once the plants have been stored in the greenhouse for the winter, we undertake the post-season preparation of the rest of the garden. In the cool days of late fall, under the first signs of winter light, we spend several days cutting the garden down. As we quietly move about the flowerbeds pruning and cleaning, it is a time of reflection. It is an amazing sight to see how much organic material gets pruned and cut from the garden each year. What we don't use for compost is hauled away, amounting to two or more pickup loads. The tiring work of cutting back the garden takes upwards of three to four days. Once the pruning has been completed, we spend the next several days spreading a layer of composted dairy manure 2 to 3 inches deep over all the beds, a practice we do once every two years. This nutrient-rich biennial top dressing protects the plants and their roots from the winter freezes, rebuilds the soil nutrients, and is the only fertilizer we use on our beds.

When the garden has been put to rest, our focus turns to storing and protecting small sculptures and water vessels. We sometimes drain the smaller water containers and, if they have a hardy water plant or lily, we remove the plants and place them in deeper holding ponds. We mark every plant with an upright stake before we submerge it so we can remember where we put it the following spring. As the cold damp days of the Northwest winter return, we find ourselves orphans of the garden and its responsibilities. We spend the next few months in the heated studio, designing and making new sculptures while planning for spring's quick return. And to renew our inspiration, we often take a holiday to Mexico so we can experience firsthand the warm air, flora, and colors of the tropics.

TIMELESSNESS
[George]

The activity of gardening is not necessarily within the realm of time. You have probably noticed that, as in all enjoyable pursuits, your being more fully present and focused seems to telescope time, maybe even reduce it to nothing. You might have been out there in the garden for hours—weeding, transplanting, planning something new, or mentally redesigning an area—and not felt them passing. That timelessness releases you and can engender a sense of well-being far greater than that which you usually experience. And, through the activities of your hands, you return that well-being to the garden itself. As it isn't a material thing, it gives visitors to the garden a sense that a mysterious presence is revealing something that is delightful but cannot be explained by thinking alone. It must, of course, be felt with the same

Amazing red veins appear on the leaves of *Hydrangea quercifolia* as it resigns itself to winter.

protecting tender plants without a greenhouse

You don't need to overlook the variety and beauty of tender and tropical plants just because you don't have a greenhouse. Many of the most adventuresome gardeners are now "pushing the envelope" of their growing zones by trying less-hardy plants and finding resourceful ways to winter them over. Potted plants can be moved inside to a sunny, airy room of the house. If you can't bring them inside for protection, place them on the south side of the house against a wall where it might be warmer. The hardiest banana, *Musa basjoo*, is a must for anyone who

wants to add a tropical look to his or her garden. This bold foliage plant can be protected with a cylindrical cage of chicken wire placed 12 inches out from the stem and then filled with straw or loose mulch to protect the tender trunks from bitter temperatures. Wrapping foil-lined house insulation around the stems of large tender plants can also offer a form of winter protection; we do this with our Tasmanian tree fern when we anticipate a hard freeze. Of course, tropicals are so exciting you could just treat them as annuals and replace them every year with wonderful newfound varieties!

Left: A true man-eater, this huge *Agave americana* awaits its new pot. **Right**: With so many variations, coleus can always be turned to for color and texture.

kind of awareness that made it, thereby encouraging people to surren-
der to the enjoyment of the moment. It gives the garden romance, in
the sense perhaps of a story to tell, or of a long history transparent in
this moment, not concerned with time. That is the magical quality that
people so love in well-made gardens. It is you, the gardener, who *are*
the garden through your good work and your love of the flora and
fauna of the place. It is you who have created in your garden the circumstances favorable to beauty.

A PEEK OVER THE FENCE
[David]

The combining of garden, art, and water comes naturally to George and me. Our eclectic style of Ancient Mediterranean, Mexican high desert, and tropical would at first seem an absurd combination, but it works. This mix of places that we are fond of, re-created in the garden and in our work, generates a balance of tranquillity and exuberance. Although our colorful, diverse style may not appeal to the faint of heart, our garden and our work are meant to awaken the creativity and adventure within us. And just as our garden is a mirror of our personalities, your garden should reflect all the qualities of your personality. Your garden style is not to be found on the pages of a book or magazine. You can use those sources to inspire and suggest, but in the process of translating their ideas to your garden they will be touched with the subtleties of your own hand. And rightly they should be. For it is all right to peek over the fence of your neighbors and be inspired—even made jealous—by their garden, but only if in doing so you arouse the spirit of adventure in your own gardening. This book was written and photographed to stimulate freethinking and a sense of playfulness. The gardening community as a whole is a very open and very giving group. There is a constant sharing of information, ideas, and plants. Like the earth of our garden, which we are constantly reworking, these bits of gifted knowledge are meant to be reworked into something of your own. And then, continuing the creative cycle, to be passed on to others.

Left: This single rheum leaf sculpture in vivid turquoise offers a striking relationship to the shapes of *Inula magnifica*'s darker leaves. **Following pages**: A view of our small entry court gives an impression of much greater space, utilizing verticals and open areas; from left, *Brugmansia, Hydrangea* 'Ayesha', a grassy-looking restio, a yucca, coral daylilies, and *Sedum* 'Autumn Joy'.

AUTHORS' ACKNOWLEDGMENTS

We wish to thank the following people who are the *sine qua non* of our life: Diane Laird who is always there for us; Maxine Steele, a lifelong source of love and inner exploration; Dan Hinkley, Robert Jones, Cynthia Sears, and Frank Buxton, our close friends and companions in travel who inspire and help us relax; Michael Gibson, dear friend and teacher whose eye for beauty is infectious; Linda Cochran, Terry Moyemont, and Terri Stanley, whose extraordinary plant knowledge and generosity helped shape our garden; Val Easton, whose prose and wit has beautifully described the feeling of our garden; and Debbi and Paul Brainerd, along with the staff and volunteers of Islandwood, who have taught us the true value of community.

The gardeners, and their gardens, who continue to inspire us: Nancy Heckler, Ciscoe and Mary Morris, Karla Waterman, Ginny Brewer, Caren Anderson, Keith and Janet Patrick, and Charles and Maryann Pember.

This book could not have been published without the assistance of the following people: Barbara Denk, whose generosity, time, and beautiful photographs gave life to this book; Kate Rogers and Karen Schober of Unleashed Book Development, who approached us one day on the ferry and set in motion the adventure of book writing, guiding us through the process with understanding and humor; Neil Maillet and the staff at Timber Press, who took a chance and gave us this extraordinary opportunity to tell our story; and Ketzel Levine, who adds zest to our life and whose foreword to our book underscores our own desire.

And finally, we'd like to acknowledge and thank all of the thousands of visitors to our garden, who have imparted their kind words and observations that inspire us and encourage us to do more.

PHOTOGRAPHER ACKNOWLEDGMENTS

My deep appreciation to George Little and David Lewis for allowing me to photograph their garden and garden art—and to witness their creative energy and spirit that brought about what I believe to be a living, breathing masterpiece.

Also, my special gratitude to Karen Schober and Kate Rogers of Unleashed Book Development, for recognizing the integrity and intimacy of my work.

And, finally: For my son Chris, with all my love, Mother.

Preceding pages: A corner of our worktable, taking color indications from nature, such as this *Epiphyllum* blossom. **Right**: The playful Barkman Fountain hidden on its own ivy-covered tree.

RESOURCES

BOOKS

An extraordinary resource for written material can be found in the Elisabeth C. Miller Library at the Center for Urban Horticulture, College of Forest Resources, University of Washington, Seattle (depts.washing ton.edu/hortlib /index.html). Some books we have found useful, however, include:

Feeney, Stephanie and Debra Prinzing. *The Northwest Gardeners' Resource Directory (9th Edition)*. Seattle, Washington: Sasquatch Books, 2002.

Hinkley, Daniel J. *The Explorer's Garden: Rare and Unusual Perennials*. Portland, Oregon: Timber Press, 1999.

Hogan, Sean. *Flora: A Gardener's Encyclopedia*. Portland, Oregon: Timber Press, 2003.

Lloyd, Christopher. *Christopher Lloyd's Garden Flowers: Perennials, Bulbs, Grasses, Ferns*. Portland, Oregon: Timber Press, 2000.

Riffle, Robert Lee. *The Tropical Look: An Encyclopedia of Dramatic Landscape Plants*. Portland, Oregon: Timber Press, 1998.

MAIL-ORDER PLANT NURSERIES

Aloha Tropicals
www.alohatropicals.com

Berkeley Horticultural Nursery
www.berkeleyhort.com

Brent and Becky's Bulbs
www.brentandbeckysbulbs.com

Cistus Nursery
www.cistus.com

Heronswood Nursery
www.heronswood.com

Plant Delights Nursery, Inc.
www.plantdelights.com

Rare Plant Research
retail.rareplantresearch.com/home.php

Stokes Tropicals
www.stokestropicals.com

Yucca Do Nursery
www.yuccado.com

Visits to the Little and Lewis garden—gallery are by appointment only. Garden clubs and organized tours are charged a nominal fee which is donated to "The Little and Lewis Endowment for the Arts at IslandWood" (www.islandwood.org). Please feel free to contact Little and Lewis at: 1940 Wing Point Way, Bainbridge Island, Washington 98110; (206) 842-8327; www.littleandlewis.com.

A large pot of nasturtiums and *Amaranth* sits high on the arbor with blue highlights of a *Musa basjoo* arching behind.

PLANT INDEX

Copyright ©2005 by Unleashed Book Development

Text © 2005 by George Little and David Lewis
Photography © 2005 by Barbara J. Denk
Foreword © 2005 by Ketzel Levine
All rights reserved.

Published in 2005 by
Timber Press, Inc.
The Haseltine Building
133 S.W. Second Avenue, Suite 450
Portland, Oregon 97204-3527, U.S.A.

Timber Press
2 Station Road
Swavesey
Cambridge CB4 5QJ, U.K.

www.timberpress.com

Reprinted 2005

ISBN 0-88192-672-8

Book design: Karen Schober
Copy editor: Alice Copp Smith
Produced by Unleashed Book Development
www.unleashedbooks.com

Page 2: A resident grass snake suns itself on a hanging tetrapanax leaf sculpture.
Pages 4–5: The small, brilliantly colored flower bract of a bromeliad hangs like a jewel, in contrast to the huge trumpet-shaped flowers of *Brugmansia*, which fill the garden with fragrance on warm evenings.
Pages 6–7 (title page): A blue Japanese glass float casts its color into the water, while a single leaf of the Plume Poppy drifts in a sphere.
Page 8: The studio table ready for work.

All photographs are by Barbara Denk, with the following exceptions: pages 56 and 100, David Lewis; page 120, Norm Plate; and page 47, courtesy Heronswood Nursery.
Hardipanel® Vertical Siding is a registered trademark of James Hardie Building Products.

Printed in China

Catalog records for this book are available from the Library of Congress and the British Library.